Stories *from* *the* Life *of* YOGANANDA

VOLUME THREE

WISDOM STORIES *series*

"Timeless Tales Told by Paramhansa Yogananda"

Stories from India, Volume One
Stories from India, Volume Two
Stories from the Life of Yogananda, Volume Three

Stories *from* *the* **Life** *of* YOGANANDA

VOLUME THREE

Paramhansa Yogananda

CRYSTAL CLARITY PUBLISHERS   Nevada City, California

CRYSTAL CLARITY PUBLISHERS
14618 Tyler Foote Rd. | Nevada City, California
crystalclarity.com | clarity@crystalclarity.com
800.424.1055

ISBN 978-1-56589-119-7 (print) | print LOC available
ISBN 978-1-56589-641-3 (e-book) | e-book LOC available

Compiled by Nayaswami Maria
Cover design by Tejindra Scott Tully
Interior design and layout by Michele Madhavi Molloy

The *Joy Is Within You* symbol is registered by Ananda
Church of Self-Realization of Nevada County, California.

Dedicated to all children of the Divine Mother

Paramhansa Yogananda

Table of Contents

Introduction

Paramhansa Yogananda delighted audiences, students, and friends with stories born of his own life experience and the people he met in his native India as well as in his global travels and cross-country American teaching campaigns. These stories are lovingly told by his direct disciple, Swami Kriyananda, his nephew, Hare Krishna Ghosh, as well as Yogananda himself.

While these stories are set in the twentieth century, they are timeless in their relevance. Addressing the age-old challenges of society at large, as well as the individual human predicament and our nature itself, these stories often give us an impersonal look at our own traits and tendencies.

Paramhansa Yogananda's stories demonstrate an expanded worldview that includes everyone. While fully engaging in the modern world of his day, he never identified with its limitations or tantalizing, illusive promises. With courage and willingness to stand up for universal truths, he shows us that we have a choice in how we are going to live and in using the inherent soul ability we possess to adapt and change, even drastically, when called upon to do so.

Each story is followed by a "Wisdom Gem" in Yogananda's own words. Giving us a clear path to conquering the limitations of ego, adjusting our attitudes, and expanding our hearts, he offers us a priceless and lasting gift that we can then share with other receptive hearts of any age.

In Divine Friendship,
Nayaswami Maria

Stories *from* *the* Life *of* YOGANANDA

VOLUME THREE

A Bunch of Grapes

Great demonstrations sometimes come from little wishes.

Once in Boston I was with a friend in a market and I saw a big bunch of fine black grapes. I wanted a bunch, but they cost $3.00, and someone who was with me said: "Isn't Swami extravagant." Hearing this remark, I decided that I would not buy the grapes. I said to myself: "The Lord knows I want them, and He will give them to me some other time."

One evening, about six months later, I entered a fruit shop and bought some grapes like those I had seen, forgetting all about the promise that God would give them to me. So, God said to me: "Return those grapes."

I turned to the storekeeper and said: "Give me a honeydew melon instead." The man looked at me puzzled, but I went out with the honeydew melon.

When I arrived home, lo, and behold, at the door was a package—a package containing *two bunches of those grapes*. There was no card attached, which made me very curious to know who had given them to me. For a month I tried to find out, when one day I heard that I would be told. As I was talking to someone, my attention was suddenly attracted to another man in the room. I asked if I could see him later, then I said to him: "God tells me that you gave me some grapes."

At first, he said: "No," but later he confessed to the following experience.

That evening, just when I was buying those grapes for myself, he was meditating, when he suddenly saw a great light and a hand holding some grapes, and the predominant thought in his mind was that he should go and buy those grapes. So, he said he bought one bunch and then another, but he still thought that the vision was hallucination. Then he prayed to be shown that it was God's vision. And that is why he bought those grapes and gave them to me.

Wisdom Gem

REAL PROSPERITY IS attained when you realize that God is your provider and that you are absolutely dependent upon Him. When you have that consciousness, you don't care what happens because you are in the immortal arms of God.

A Changed Life

One evening, at Carnegie Hall, he inspired a full house to chant Guru Nanak's song, "He Hari Sundara," in English: "O God Beautiful." For one hour and a half they chanted that song, uplifted by Yogananda's magnetism to a state that verged on ecstasy. Later, streaming out into the streets, their faces were wreathed in blissful smiles: a rare sight in that city!

The Master was in his interview room afterward, when a tough-looking gangster-type burst into the room and flung a revolver down on the desk. Emotionally he cried: "I could kill you for what you've done to me this evening! I can't go back to that way of life anymore!"

Yogananda looked at him kindly, then said, "No, you can't go back, because now you know why you committed yourself to that way in the first place: You thought the money you'd earn from crime would make you happy. Now you know it never will!"

The man began sobbing. "Oh! Let me feel that bliss you talked about! My heart has been a desert! Now, all I want is bliss!"

"Dear child of God!" Yogananda spoke compassionately. "Even if you turn your back on Him, He loves you always. Try now to see Him in all. When death comes, you will soar upward in His light!"

The man hunched over the desk, still sobbing. His whole life-direction had been changed.

Wisdom Gem

YOGANANDA'S WAY OF loving was very different from what you might think. It was not a sweet sentiment or a gentle expression. It was that kind of power that could oppose evil, but with love and respect. Master had that kind of power and wisdom in his love that was always working for your true welfare. When you feel the power of that love, it's shattering. It will shatter all your false preconceptions of what life's all about. It will show you that life is altogether different from what you thought it was, and that all the things that you thought were so important aren't at all. They're just dust.

A Great Failure Who Became a Great Success

As there are naturally successful people, so there are also habitual failures. John, my friend and student, was such a born failure. He was young, intelligent, and diligent, but it seemed that no matter what job or business he tried, he failed. Harassed, deserted, and penniless, he sought my advice.

He said: "Sir, I am a great failure. For some mysterious reason, not only do I lose my job, but also, after employing me, my employer loses his business. I hate to seek a job for fear of destroying the business of my new employer through the deathly grip of my failure vibration. I am labeled a failure by all of my friends, and I thoroughly believe that I can never succeed."

Through my influence, John got a job in a small business concern. I advised him to affirm daily, before going to bed and upon waking, "Day by day, in every way, I am succeeding more and more in my job."

A month passed and John warned me: "Honored Sir, the business concern you got me into is getting into worse and worse trouble. Please remove me before it goes onto the rocks completely. Perhaps my resignation will save the business from destruction."

I laughed and told John to keep up his affirmation of success and to hold on to his job. After a fortnight John came to me one evening and, with a sigh of relief, exclaimed, "It happened." I asked, "What happened?" "Well, my employer's business collapsed, as I told you it would."

I turned to John and remonstrated: "Every night and every morning, while you have been mentally parroting the affirmation, 'Day by day I am getting better and better,' in the background of your mind, a little octopus of obstinacy has kept on repeating, 'You simpleton, you know that day by day, in every way, you are getting worse and worse.'" He admitted the truth of this.

Smilingly, I reminded John to cast out all negative vibrations during a positive affirmation, because a convinced, conscious mind influences the subconscious, which in turn influences the conscious mind through the power of habit.

I told John that his success was conditioned by his creative ability, his environment, and his prenatal and postnatal habits, and that if he contacted the all-powerful superconscious mind, then alone could he create the cause for absolute success.

I succeeded in getting John a job in another and bigger business. After six months (the longest period he'd ever held a job), he said to me, "Sir, get me out quick. Business is getting pretty bad."

I paid no attention to John's misgivings and told him to go on with his job. After a few weeks, John smilingly moaned, "Sir, the second business you got me into has evaporated too." I pretended to feel sorrowful at his plight, and calmly said, "Never mind, John, I will get you another job."

"Well, Sir," he said, "If you can bear the sin of causing other peoples' businesses to collapse through contact with me, then find me another job."

By continuous effort and influence, I at last secured for John a good job in a very big concern. A year passed and nothing happened, although almost every week John wanted to give up his job, fearing that he would cause the collapse of this third business.

Finally, I asked John to invest his money in a business of his own. He was beside himself with fear, and shouted at me, "If I invest the money I have saved, I am sure to lose it." I firmly assured him: "Of course you must invest your money and energy in some good project, like order-supplying of stationery, which requires no large investment or overhead. I am sure you will succeed."

In the course of a few years, John found himself owning a few successful chain stores and a large amount of capital.

When John was thoroughly convinced of his success, he found himself succeeding in

everything he undertook. One day he laughingly said: "Through God and through your help, I
am changed from a great failure to a great success. Please tell me how this happened. I can
understand my own failure owing to lack of understanding, but I cannot understand how I de-
molished other peoples' businesses by the power
of my failure vibration."

I replied: "You did not destroy the businesses you were in. The law of attraction that governs
people of like vibrations was at work. You attracted a business about to fail, and vice versa, like two
lighted bombs rolling down the hill side by side.
You were a failure and the business was about to
fail. By the law of inner affinity, you went down
the hill of failure together and exploded at the
same time."

The Western brothers must learn that the mind
is greater than its inventions. More time should be
given to the art of controlling the mind for scientifically achieving all-round success. Less time
should be spent pursuing the products of mind
at the cost of neglecting the cultivation of the all-
accomplishing, all-powerful mind itself. Follow
the way taught by India of acquiring superconsciousness and absolute control over the mind,
and thus learn to create at will what you need.

Wisdom Gem

MIND IS THE source of all your troubles and all your happiness. You are stronger than all your tests. Use constructively the power you already have, and more will come. Tune yourself with Cosmic Power. Then you will possess the creative power of Spirit. You will be in contact with Infinite Intelligence, which can guide you and solve all problems. Power from the dynamic Source of your being will flow through you so that you will be creative in the world of business, the world of thought, or the world of wisdom.

Called to America

C ome here, Bimal!" Yogananda cried gaily. "I have news for you. The Lord is calling me to America!"

Inwardly, then, he said to God, "So then, my work here is finished."

Bimal as a two-legged newspaper did his work well. By the time the youthful headmaster emerged from that storage room, the whole school had been apprised of the news. A few of the newer teachers said jokingly, "So, shall we carry lanterns ahead of you, to light your way into those dark regions?"

Yogananda replied, "Don't joke about it. I am going today, by the three o'clock train to Calcutta." Everyone wondered where he would find the necessary funding. He had been receiving no salary. He had no "counting house" full of gold coins. He was, in fact, more or less penniless.

That same day, however, he left for Calcutta. How amazingly sudden was this decision! That

vision had come to him between ten and eleven
o'clock in the morning. He entrained for Calcutta
at three o'clock that same day! Before leaving he
had to pack, appoint others to take his place, give
them last-minute instructions and advice, then
say goodbye to the whole student body.

Thus began the next, and most important,
phase of his life: his mission to the West. After his
arrival in Calcutta he told his latest news to everyone he knew. A college teacher named Bhajan
came to him that very afternoon and said, "Do
you know, the principal of my college, Haramba
Maitro, will be going to a conference in Boston,
Massachusetts, in September. It will be a congress
of religious liberals, sponsored by the Unitarian
Universalist Church."

Yogananda replied, "You really must take me
to him."

The principal selected him as the representative
to that congress for the organization Yogananda
had founded to create his school in Ranchi. And
thus was the ball set in motion.

Yogananda went next to Serampore to see his
guru. "Is this all true, Master?" he asked. "Am I
really supposed to go?"

"Yes," replied the great guru. "It is now or never.
All paths are open to you."

Yogananda returned to Calcutta. The next evening, a friend came over and told him of someone he knew who was also going to America. This

person came over, and said, "I'll introduce you to a man at the shipping office."

At the shipping office, the man said, "There is no space available. Everything is fully booked for the next six months."

Yogananda said, "I'll be leaving anyway." The ship, *The City of Sparta*, was scheduled to sail the next month.

"There's simply no berth available," the clerk replied.

Yogananda's reply was the same: "I'll be sailing on it."

The clerk (an Englishman) now lost his temper. He shouted, "You can't even get a passport in so little time! The police will need a full six months to investigate you." India under the English had its own special difficulties.

"That's all right," the youthful swami replied. "I'll be sailing on that ship. Perhaps someone will cancel his booking."

"There's not a chance!" shouted the clerk angrily. He wrote Yogananda's name on his shirt cuff with a copying pencil. My guru commented later, "He didn't know it, but that action ruined his shirt!" Why the man wrote Yogananda's name at all I simply don't know. Perhaps it was to record Yogananda as an applicant, despite his assurance that there was no hope. Or perhaps he was just reminding himself to have nothing more to do with this human gadfly!

Two days later, Yogananda wanted to return there. "This time I won't join you!" his friend said. "You almost came to blows!"

"No," the young swami replied. "I was only asserting myself!" Now, however, he went instead to the police, and there he requested a passport.

"Impossible!" they replied. "With the war so newly ended, everyone is under suspicion. To investigate you adequately will take us at least three months." *The City of Sparta* was the first steamer scheduled to depart from Calcutta since the end of World War I.

Later that very day, Yogananda's father said that a relative of theirs, an uncle, was in the next room. This man was a deputy magistrate. When the uncle understood his nephew's predicament, he said, "I'll see that you get your passport right away." And Yogananda thought, "As my guru said, all paths are open."

In a very short time, the passport was in his hands. He now returned to the shipping office. The clerk wouldn't even look at him. The young swami coughed to get his attention, then said to him, "Come here."

"Where is your passport?"

"Where is my berth?"

"Where is your passport?"

"Where is my berth?"

"All right, yes, we do have a cancellation, but it's for a berth you couldn't possibly afford. It's in first class."

"Who says I can't afford it? Write me down for that berth."

Yogananda hadn't the money. He possessed hardly a rupee. Confidently, however, he produced his passport. The man's jaw dropped. "All right," he said, "but you'll have to give me that advance deposit."

"I'll go back for it."

His father said to him, "Don't expect me to give you this money. I don't even want you to go!"

"But God wants me to go."

"Well, the money won't come from me!"

"That's all right. I didn't ask you."

The next day, his father, before he went out to work, left a check with another child of his, a daughter, telling her, "I was wrong to deny Mukunda that money. God has told me to give him this check." The check was enough to cover the cost of the cabin, leaving some for further expenses besides. When Yogananda next saw his father, he said, "Father, I can't take this money from you. I don't want you to feel coerced."

His father replied, "No, it was God who changed my mind. This money comes not from me as your father, but from a faithful disciple of Lahiri Mahasaya." He then wept. "Will you ever return?" he asked.

"I'll come back in three months," replied his son, "if the Americans don't need me. It all depends on their interest and need." Well, we all know the sequel to that.

Wisdom Gem

A STRONG WILL, by its dynamic force, creates a way for its fulfillment. By its very strength, the will sets into motion certain vibrations in the atmosphere. Nature, with its laws of order, system, and efficiency, then creates circumstances favorable to the individual who exercises will power. Will derives its strength from an honest purpose, lofty motives, and the noble concern to do good for the world at large. A strong will is never stifled—it always finds a way.

Death and the Dream

Mind is the wool with which the cloth of Creation is woven. Mind was frozen into matter. A dream is the temporary frozen fancy of man. Creation is the comparatively more lasting frozen fancy of God. Without mind, matter, sensation, thought, and feelings, Nature is impossible to be cognized. In a dream, the mind plays the part of the material objects as well as the conscious creatures in the dream.

In a dream, the mind materializes itself into the earth, sunlight, flowers, rivers, mountains, glens, oceans, sky, air, fire, ether, and water. In that dream setting of the earth, the mind materializes itself into sentient blossoms, singing birds, and conscious human beings.

While in a dream, you perceive the earth you walk on as different from the water in which you might be swimming, and you breathe the air, feel the heat of the sun, smell the fragrance of flowers, feel cool and heat, and have all kinds of sensations. In a dream, you see a baby born, a person die, and someone sick, and someone healthy. In a dream, you think, feel, will, hate, love, forgive, or are revengeful, or are happy or sad, rich or poor, or become a rich business man or a poverty-stricken man.

While you are dreaming, you recognize the relative difference between solids, liquids, gases, water, air, ether, fire, thought, feeling, will, sadness, joy, poverty, prosperity, health, sickness, birth, and death, but upon waking you see no difference between solids, liquids, gases, ether, thought, birth, death, darkness, light, sadness, and happiness, for they are all the different rates of vibrating mind. Darkness is a thought different from the thought called "light." So birth is a thought different from the thought called "death." Sad thoughts are different from happy thoughts, but sadness and happiness are both different rates of vibrating thought. Happiness is soothing thought; sadness is burning thought.

Once I sat meditating deeply. I was very much puzzled as to the difference between matter and mind, then the Lord sent me a vision. I beheld myself in the midst of a battle. As the Captain of a fighting cruiser, I was ordering rapid cannon fire from near the shore, over the enemy assembled on the shore, and gunning our battleship. My sailors were killed and my ship was riddled with cannon balls. At last, a great shell burst a huge leak in the vessel and it started sinking.

I plunged headlong into the water with a gun dangling on my back. I felt the cool water splash around me as I jumped. Then I swam ashore, and as I was running toward the jungle near the shore, I met a company of armed soldiers, who leveled their guns to shoot me. I became tired of fighting and swimming, so I raised my hands in surrender, but it was too late. A fiery bullet-dart pierced my heart and I crumpled to the earth, bleeding profusely.

I remember vividly all the sensations attending death. I felt the sensation of losing all sensations. I felt that I had lungs, but I could not breathe or feel the motion of the diaphragm. I wanted to move my tongue and feel the sensation of taste, but I could not do so. I felt that I had eyes, but I could not see; I felt that I had ears, but I could not hear. My body, heart, hands, and limbs lay paralyzed and went to sleep. It was just as you might see your leg and know that it was yours, but you could not move it, when it went to sleep, so I felt that I had my body and all my limbs and organs, but they all went to sleep and would not move in response to my violently-urging will.

Then I thought to myself: "This is the famous death of which I heard so much about while I lived on earth. After all, it was not so bad, due to the absence of all physical pain, only I was in mental agony because I was sure that I had a body but could not use it. My body lay motionless, inert, as experienced in a nightmare, not responding to the call of my will in the slightest degree. At last, when I was convinced that I was dead, and knowing that I could not do anything with my bodily engine, which had completely gone dead, I resolved to relax my will to live, so I roamed away in the Infinite ether.

Just at this time, as I was sadly soaring away out of the body, like a vapor of light, suddenly the Lord returned to me the consciousness of my body fully alive, and I was resting on the bedstead meditating. My joy was boundless. I touched my body all over to make sure that I had hands and feet which I could move. I breathed in and out a hundred times to make sure that I could use my lungs. I felt my heart-throbs on the palm of my hand placed over my breast, to make sure that I was living again. I was bewildered and beside myself with joy, almost hysterical, to feel that I was alive again. I thanked the Lord again and again that I was permitted to return from the land "from whose bourne no traveler returns." I was glad to return from the land of the dead to the land of the living. Suddenly, as I was in the height of glee at finding myself alive instead of being stone-dead, with a bullet wound, I realized, with great horror, that I apparently was stone-dead again. I had bled to death with a bullet in my heart.

This strange vision of life and death kept alternately coming and going several times within me. When I saw myself alive, I was convinced that was true, only that became falsified when I saw myself dead again, and was convinced that I was dead. When I saw myself alive, the vision of death was false, and when I saw myself dead, the vision of life was untrue. Puzzled, I cried, when I found myself alive, and prayed to be shown if I had lost my mind. When the Lord appeared to me in a human body, I bowed and said: "Lord, tell me! Which is true: Am I alive or am I dead?"

The Lord replied: "You are seemingly both alive and dead, but your dream of life and death both are false. This world is My dream. When I dream life, you see yourself alive, and when I dream death, you see your body dead. Now awaken in My consciousness, uninterrupted by this seeming change of life and death, and know that you were never born and never died, but are alive in Me forever and forever."

Wisdom Gem

WAKE UP TO the one Reality, God, and you will see that this earth life is just a show. It is nothing but shadows and light! Everything exists only in consciousness.

Ever-New Joy

My **Master once** said to me: "The spiritual aspirant who tries to fly the clutches of material attachments, often in delusion, wants them in the form of miracles. Therefore, in trying to get away from matter, do not deceive yourself and invite matter in another subtle form. If all the miraculous powers and material possessions are given to you, you will nevertheless remain dissatisfied by growing tired of that which you have received. There is only one thing that you will never become tired of, if you once have it. Peace is the altar of Joy. You will never become tired of Joy. Ever-changing, ever-lasting, ever-new Joy is God—you will become tired of everything except ever-new Joy."

Instead of looking for God in the chambers of mystery, sky, and beauty; instead of keeping Him aloof in a certain distant spot, through Master's direction I silently cried within myself continuously: "Come! Come!" In the Temple of Joy I always heard Him reply in the echo of my love: "I am here! I am here!"

Instead of waiting during many lives in order to meet God, I plunged headlong and swam within myself, and lo! I found Him hiding within me. I found that forgetfulness and dark indifference were the veils which hid me from Him. I tore asunder those veils and discovered that my memory and my love for Him were doors to His Presence. As often as I thought of Him, the door flung open and I felt His Presence. The memory of God is the altar of God's Presence. Whenever you think of Him, you manifest His Omnipresence within you.

One day I was meditating with another boy and I said: "Today we shall see the great Prophet Krishna." We had started meditating early in the morning and went on and on, and finally the other boy said: "Let us go to bed now." I said: "No, we are going to see Krishna." We kept on meditating for another hour and then the other boy said: "We won't see anything, let us go to bed." I said: "No, I shall stay here until I see the Prophet Krishna," and as I spoke suddenly the Prophet Krishna appeared in a vision. Oh, it was beautiful! He was walking on a sea of gold. The other boy saw it also for just a flash of a second.

So, remember, if you make up your mind, and you know that nothing can hold you back, then how can you help but be successful? You are using your will power in the wrong way when you make up your mind that you cannot be successful.

Wisdom Gem

YOU ARE MOVING to the Palace of Joy. You are traveling by the quickest path of meditation. The path is beautiful as you advance farther and farther along. You will come across many beautiful gardens of mental miracles. Do not be sidetracked and become bewitched by the seeming beauty of these blooming mental powers. Do not inhale their poisonous charm by displaying these miracles, for in that case you will be left by the wayside, loving only dominion over matter. Thus, in order to leave the territory of matter, you are lured in its domain by another false pretext. Tarry not, forsake powers which promise charm and happiness now for a moment, only to throw you into continuous suffering in the end. Rather, seek the permanent charm of the Palace of Joy which will come to you in the end, perhaps after a series of troublesome difficult efforts. If you wait, beholding only the beauty of the garden of powers, you will never reach the home of Joy—the fountain from which all powers come.

Fads, Diets, Science, and Common Sense

n Los Angeles, a diet fad group served what they called "unfired foods." Because Yogananda was a vegetarian — an uncommon thing for Americans in those days — and because he was famous, this group invited him to a "sort of" banquet, at which they hoped he would also speak.

"They took me proudly through their kitchen," he said later. "Everything I saw there seemed designed to awaken distaste!

"Later, they led me to their dining room and served me the 'feast' they'd prepared. Carrots, carrots, and more carrots! I was able to get some of it down!

"After this ordeal, they asked me to speak to them and their guests. I demurred.

"'Oh, please say just a few words.'

"'I really don't think you'd like what I have to say,' I replied.

"'Oh, come now! You must have enjoyed what we fed you. You *must* say something.'

"'Very well,' I said. 'Forgive me, but I must be truthful. To begin with, the meal I have just eaten is the most tasteless I have ever had in my life.'

"'Oh, for shame! It was wonderfully healthful.'

"'Food, to be healthful, should also please the palate. But that is my next point: You all consider it healthful, but it was seriously lacking in important dietary ingredients.'

"'You're wrong!' they shouted. 'It was completely scientific!'

"'No. It's as though you took pride in punishing yourselves. But I warn you, unless you change your ways, in fifteen days one of you will die of malnutrition.'

"Well, they were outraged, and refused even to listen to me further. Fifteen days later, one of their members did die of malnutrition. The police came in, and closed their entire establishment."

Wisdom Gem

OBEY THE MATERIAL laws of the body by a sensible choice of food. Since you have to eat, eat the right kind of food. Choose a balanced diet, stick to it, and then forget the body; devote your time to the more important studies and problems of life.

Faith vs Carelessness

Two ladies that I knew had a habit of leaving their car unlocked when they parked it. I once said to them, "You should take the precaution of locking your car."

"What's the matter with you?" they cried. "Where is your faith in God?"

"I have faith," I answered, "but this is not faith you are exercising. It is carelessness. Why should God protect you, when you won't do anything to protect yourselves?"

"Oh, the Lord watches over us," they assured me. "Nothing will be stolen." So they kept on leaving their car as if half locked, but half open.

Well, one day they had several thousand dollars' worth of bonds and other rare possessions in their car. They went off, leaving everything in the charge of their vaunted "faith." During their absence, thieves came and stole everything, with the exception of a minor item they'd somehow overlooked. One of the ladies lost all the money she'd been saving for years.

Later I said to them, "Why expect God to protect you if you ignore His laws of reason and common sense? Have faith, but at the same time be practical. Don't make unnecessary demands of God, nor expect Him to do everything for you just because you believe in Him. He will take care of you, but you must also do your share."

Wisdom Gem

FAITH MEANS EXPANDING your intuitive aware-
ness of God's presence within, and not relying on
reason as your chief means of understanding.

I Am God

The goal of yoga is to merge in the Infinite and in that state to realize that God is you. You cannot say "I am God." That would be wrong because that would be saying that the little wave of manifestation is the whole ocean. That's not true. Any yogi who says "I am God" is speaking an untruth. But you can say, "I am the wave. He is the ocean. He is me. He is my little wave of manifestation." This you can say. And you can go on to say that that wave of manifestation is He.

One time Yogananda came to this saint, he was a boy at that time, and the saint saw his great humility and devotion so, in front of all his disciples he said, "I am God." My Guru leapt to his feet and he showed him a mirror and he said, "You don't say so! This isn't the God I am looking for!" and he walked out in great indignation. Well, the saint came running after him and prostrated himself and said, "Thank you. You have awakened me from a great delusion."

And he had the humility to do this and to apologize in front of all his devotees but Yogananda answered him, and his name was Mukunda then, and he answered him and said that, "It is not right to say the wave is the ocean, but you can say the ocean has become all of its waves." So you can't say, "I am God," but you can say God has become this little being. That is true, and when you reach that state, that is what you will be.

Wisdom Gem

IT SEEMS SO impossible to believe right now, I mean here you are wanting things and getting angry with people, being afraid of this, and hungry for that and so on, and so on. This is not you. You are just a bundle of self-definitions as long as you live in this little ego. And once you've understood that those definitions are not you, you shed that bundle and you become a *jivan mukta* [free while living].

Money Won't Give You
Happiness

A man whom **Paramhansa** Yogananda met in New York complained to him, "I can never forgive myself for taking thirty-five years to make my first million dollars!"

"You still are not satisfied?" inquired the Master.

"Far from it!" lamented the businessman. "A friend of mine has made several times that. Now I won't be happy until I've made forty million!"

Paramhansa Yogananda, recalling this episode years later, ended his account of it by saying, "Before that man could make his forty million and settle down to spending the rest of his days in peace and happiness, he suffered a complete nervous breakdown. Soon afterwards, he died.

"Such is the fruit of excessive worldly ambition."

Wisdom Gem

A MATERIALISTIC LIFE tempts mankind with smiles and assurances, but is consistent only in this: It never fails, eventually, to break all its promises.

Mistaken Identity

Spiritual introspection and perception of intellectually studied truth both reinforce the Infinite source from which all intelligence comes. Through meditation and intuitive perception you get more intellectual truths than through reading books. For best results, turn your intelligence to your intuition after meditation. What cannot be perceived through the senses, cannot be inferred about through the reason. "Then how do I know I exist," you ask? From direct perception of your intuition and not through the intermediary faculties of sensory perceptions and reason.

Once I went to a farmhouse and met a man who had semi-developed intuition. He bothered everybody with the display of his intuition. He tried it on me several times, until I had an overdose of his semi-intuitional practices and decided to wake him up.

One day, while we were sitting in the farm parlor and the door was closed, we heard footsteps, and I asked my semi-intuitive friend:

"Will you please tell me who is at the door?"

He forthwith replied: "It is my uncle coming home after many years, and he never even wrote me about it."

The door was opened and the uncle appeared, and when questioned he verified the statement, and said that he came suddenly without notification. My friend triumphantly exclaimed:

"See, I have fully-developed intuition and not semi-developed intuition as you often say."

Then I remonstrated: "My friend, beware, you will make a horrible blunder some time, because you have had a little intuition all your life, but you have not practiced the technique of developing it to the extent that you can really depend upon it." He laughed at me, but soon I had the occasion to laugh at him. My mischievous prayer was answered.

One dismal, rainy day, we sat in the farm parlor again, when suddenly there was a loud knock on the closed door. I said to my friend: "Now use your semi-intuition and tell me who is knocking."

He concentrated for a moment, then said: "My brother has unexpectedly arrived. Open the door."

I laughed at him and replied: "No, not I. I wouldn't go near the door; my intuition tells me not to. You had better open the door yourself."

Saying this, I ran to the other side of the room. He opened the door, and in rushed the farm bull with menacing horns, angrily seeking shelter from the rain. My friend jumped aside frantically and the bull ran after me. Of course, I was prepared for it and just stepped aside, loudly exclaiming: "My friend, your semi-intuition indeed foretold about your brother arriving."

Wisdom Gem

INTUITION MUST BE distinguished from self-confidence, from the superstition of "Because it happened so many times, consequently it will happen always," and from "overworked confidence." There are many psychological upstarts which pose as intuition and delude people. Real Intuition can never be wrong. Only when wrong psychological states are mistaken for intuition, do they bring trouble.

My Experience with an Orthodox Believer in Hell-Fire

On another occasion, in the Pacific Northwest, Yogananda stopped at a farmhouse hoping to buy some cherries, and got into a discussion on religion with the farmer. At a certain point this man, who proved to be a religious fanatic, shouted, "We are all sinners!—and the Lord will burn our souls in hell-fire and brimstone!"

The Master paused a moment before replying. Then he asked, as if irrelevantly, "You have a son, haven't you?"

The other answered dolefully, "Yes. I have a son."

"He gives you trouble, doesn't he?"

"Oh, my God, what trouble!"

"He drinks, I think?"

"Like a whale! You can't imagine the grief I go through on his account."

Yogananda then announced confidently, "I have a cure for his problem."

"Oh, sir, if you can help me with that, I'll be grateful to you forever!"

"Well, here's what you do: The next time he comes home late at night, drunk . . ." He interrupted himself.

"Have you a large oven?"

The man glared suspiciously. "Say," he demanded, "what have you got in mind?"

"No, no, just wait." Yogananda spoke reassuringly. "I'm offering you a solution to your problem."

Hesitantly the man replied, "Yes, I have such an oven."

"Has it a large door?"

Suddenly again apprehensive, the man cried, "Just a minute! Where is all this heading?"

The Master spoke soothingly. "Just be calm. I'm going to solve everything for you."

The other sat back, relaxing slightly.

"Now then, here's what you do: The next time your son comes home drunk. . . well, first, have the oven good and hot . . ."

The man sat up again, horrified.

Yogananda was now speaking hurriedly: "Grab him; tie him up with a strong rope, and shove him into the oven!"

Furiously indignant, the man shouted, "Blasphemer! Evildoer! Whoever heard of a father throwing his own son into an oven! Get out of my house this minute!"

Yogananda then spoke appeasingly. "Don't you understand what I've just said to you? You said God wants to throw us all into hell. But He is our true Father! You, a mere human being, were horrified at the thought of throwing your own son into an oven despite all the trouble he's given you. How could you think the Divine Father, who has infinitely greater love than you, and who created parental love, would burn His own children with hell-fire and brimstone?"

The old man's eyes filled with tears of repentance as he said, "I see now." He reflected a moment. "Yes, you are right." He looked at his visitor with a grateful smile. "Oh, thank you! You've cured me of a serious error. I understand now that the Heavenly Father is a God of love. He *can't* wish our destruction! Thank you! Thank you!"

Wisdom Gem

GOD LOVES YOU just as much as He loves Krishna, Jesus, and the other great masters. You are a drop of the same ocean of Spirit. For the ocean is made up of all its drops. You are a part of God. You were given your importance by the Lord Himself. You are His very own.

My Pet Deer

In God there is no separation, but for those who have not realized the Oneness of God, there is separation and death. They see a blank wall of death into which souls are dumped and are gone and forgotten, but the person of Realization sees beyond the land of death, where all souls are dancing and awaking again. Death should not cause sorrow. Oh, how sad I used to feel when friends passed away. You must not feel this way. When you know God, you will see everyone in the Great Divine; then you will realize that they are really never away from you.

Once, in India, I became very fond of a little deer. I had seen one being fed with a little bottle and I said to myself: "How I would like to have a little deer like that one." Then one day, long after, I told my friends that God was going to give me a deer. So it happened one day, as I was bathing in the river, when the children came running and said: "We have a deer," I ran out of the water and there was my deer, and I tell you that deer used to sleep in my room and come near my bed. How I loved it!

One day I was going away from the school and I told one of the students not to feed the deer for I feared something serious would happen if he did. I had gotten that feeling while chanting earlier in the day. But, sad to relate, he bought a bottle of milk and gave it all to the deer at one feeding, and the deer almost passed out. I almost died with sorrow when I returned. I said, "If there is a God, He will not take my deer away." So I began to meditate, and after three hours the deer got up. God had given him back to me.

But what a lesson I learned later! I never forgot it. As the deer began to walk, I said to the boy, "I told you there was danger. Why did you feed him?"

I stayed up until 2 o'clock and the deer was still alive. I felt a little sleepy, so decided to go to bed. Strange to say, I didn't even put the deer in my room that evening, but put it in a room next to mine, and thus I fell asleep. But at 3 o'clock the form of my deer appeared to me and said, "You are holding me back. Let me go! Let me go!" I said: "All right." Then suddenly I awakened and said: "The deer is dying." Then the whole school awakened. The deer made a last effort to get up, walked toward me, then dropped at my feet dead.

I learned a lesson that night. The karma (law of cause and effect) of the deer was over. It was to go, but I was holding it because of my attachment.

I was selfish in not wanting the deer to go on to a higher state of development. I was holding it in the body when the soul was struggling to get out of that little form. So the deer's actual soul came to ask release, and until I gave permission it wouldn't or couldn't go, but as soon as I said, "All right," then it went.

Wisdom Gem

GOD MEANS FOR you to love everything and see everything in Him, but if you are attached, then you see only death. The man who is attached sees the curtain fall at death, but when he is not attached, but loves with the love of God, then at death he realizes that he has only gone back to God.

Never Call Yourself a Sinner

In Los Angeles, Yogananda once went to a revival meeting. A woman was leading it. (I have always assumed that it was the famous woman evangelist Aimee Semple McPherson, but I don't really know.) During her harangue she shouted: "God has no use for sinners! In His eyes they are an abomination!"

Voices were raised everywhere in fervent response: "Hallelujah! Praise the Lord! Right on, Sister!"

"Unless you accept Jesus Christ, and live for his glory, you will end up in hell!"

Again the responses, with a few variations.

The woman continued, "Man is naturally sinful. He can be redeemed only by faith in our Lord, Jesus Christ!"

Once more the congregation intoned heartfelt replies.

"You are all sinners! Get down on your knees!"

In all that crowd, only Yogananda remained standing. Later, he commented, "I wouldn't accept her statement that I was a sinner! Nobody should ever say that. To call yourself a sinner is the greatest of all sins before God! Don't identify yourself with your mistakes. When you know God, you will become aware of His presence everywhere. And then you will never judge anyone."

Wisdom Gem

THE WORST SIN is to call yourself a sinner. For in that very thought you open the door, and invite sin to enter your mind. Never dwell on the thought of your shortcomings. Recall, instead, the memory of the good things you have done, and of the goodness that exists in the world. Convince yourself of your own innate perfection. Thus you will find yourself drawn to remember your eternal nature as a child of God.

Open Your Bank Book
with God

Several years ago, when I was on the train going to Los Angeles, I met a man whose manner and general appearance immediately attracted my attention. He was a well-dressed, prosperous looking business man, with every indication that he was blessed with all the good things of life and had every reason to be happy, but regardless of all these favorable outward impressions, for some reason I felt very sorry for him, because he radiated so much gloom. I said to myself, "What is the matter with this man, I must resurrect him. He has buried himself beneath this artificial habit of gloom."

I looked straight at him and said: "Are you happy?" He tried to annihilate me with a fierce look, but I looked straight at him again with the thought, what have I to fear? Nothing.

Finally, he said, "Is that your business?" I said, "Yes, to resurrect the walking dead." I thought that he had already killed me in his mind and he could not kill me again.

He said, "Yes, I am happy." I said, "No, I can tell what is in the mind." I call a spade a spade. He said, "Why shouldn't I be happy? I put fifty to sixty thousand dollars a month in the bank." I thought, "Poor soul!"

I said, "Tomorrow you may not be here to carry a cent. Have you opened your bank book with God?"

Later he invited me to lunch, but he was inwardly antagonistic to me. Then we talked again and he became more reasonable.

I said, "Do not rely on riches. You may die and not even have a chance to make a will. These material riches are not yours. Open your bank book with God."

He said, "Meet me in Boston." I said, "Meet me in Los Angeles." But he did not have time. Then later, when in Boston, I was at the hotel where he stopped and the hotel manager said, "Don't you know what happened to him? He was coming from a hockey match and was struck down by a truck and never regained consciousness." I felt very badly. Do you see, he woke up a little bit, but not enough.

If you have insurance with the Infinite, you will know whether or not Nature shatters your body, that you are still on the lap of immortality, still on the lap of that Infinite assurance. Resurrect yourself from the consciousness of human habits and the human thoughts thereof. Live every second in that consciousness. It is the last thing, that alone which will live forever. This is not to frighten you, but to quicken your understanding, to quicken your efforts—that you do not keep your soul buried under false satisfaction.

Wisdom Gem

OPEN YOUR BANK book with Him—it will never be lost. You can use it through all your travels now and in eternity, whether in an airplane or an astral plane. You should say to yourself: "From star to star I will fly, whether on this side of eternity, or the other side of eternity, or whether surging through the waves of life, from atom to atom— flying with the lights, whirling with the stars, or dancing with human lives! I am an immortal! I have resurrected myself from the consciousness of death.

Overcoming Anger

When I was a boy, I liked to play football. In one of the neighborhoods we moved to, the boys cursed and used vulgar language. I didn't care for it, so I said, "As long as you talk like that, I won't come and play with you." That led them to decide that we were enemies.

One day they hatched a plot to punish me. There was a crazy fellow who lived in our neighborhood; people called him "Jotin, the mad fellow." He would pick a fight with anyone, even without any reason. Those boys threatened to set him on me if I refused to play with them. Still I said, "I won't come so long as you go on using foul language."

Well, the following evening this man was waiting for me in the park through which I passed every day. I saw him even before entering the park. He was carrying a big stick in his hand. There were two friends of mine walking with me; they said, "Don't go in there. He means to give you a big beating." I answered, "Don't be afraid. We can go in."

First, however, I returned to my room and meditated. There I prayed to Shiva, Lord of Destruction. "Let my love and blessings destroy Jotin's anger!"

I then returned to the park. My friends wouldn't join me. Jotin blocked the path, menacingly brandishing his stick. I walked up to him slowly, and looked him straight in the eye, calmly and steadily. There ensued a pause. Then he dropped his gaze, smiled a little sheepishly, and left the scene.

That next night, in meditation, I asked Shiva to change Jotin. In the afternoon of the following day, I went back to the park. Jotin was standing there; this time, however, there was no stick in his hand. Evening was falling, and Jotin began to follow me. My friends, who had come with me, whispered fearfully, "He is coming this way. He intends to beat you up." They hurried away. When Jotin caught up with me, however, he prostrated on the ground before me and cried, "What have you done to me? Shiva appeared before me in a vision last night, and said to me, 'You are being unjust.'" He added, "I want to follow you." Thus, he became my student.

A few months later, he said to me one day, "You have helped me in so many ways—God, through you. Can you help me in my present predicament? Every time my boss scolds me, I become angry and slap him. Owing to this weakness of mine, I can't hold a job. But I just can't help myself. I lose my temper too easily."

I said to him, "I have taught you meditation. Tonight, while meditating, keep these words in mind: Whatever thought you hold strongly, surround it with energy, and let it wash away the habit you wish to destroy."

Jotin did as I'd suggested. He practiced this simple technique daily for weeks. One day, he came and told me gratefully, "Mukunda, I have overcome my anger."

I decided he needed to be tested. He too, after all, had to be sure in himself that the change was firmly established. Recalling the many enemies he'd made, I told a few of them to do everything they could to make him angry. They gave it a good try! However, they failed. Jotin never faltered for a moment. He had, indeed, overcome his anger.

Wisdom Gem

IF YOU ARE able to free yourself from bad habits, and if you are able to do good because you want to do good and because doing evil will bring you sorrow, then you are truly progressing. It is only when you discard your bad habits that you are a free individual.

Path of Success:
A Personal Account

I loved philosophy and religion from my boy-
hood, and I made up my mind to establish my own
schools and institutions and never hold a job under anybody. It would have been folly on my part
to become a railroad man, as was planned for me.
I started on my path with infinite confidence that I
would succeed, and I did succeed. My success was
due to strong determination, and confidence in
the guidance of the Heavenly Father in everything
I undertook. My effectiveness came through God
and creative thinking principally, and very little
through human training.

As I headed toward my goal, I tried to succeed
in different lines of endeavor. When I saw that I
succeeded in all the things I undertook, then I
fully launched myself into the greatest undertak-
ing of my life—Spiritual Organization. I started
my first work in a little mud hut with three or
four others in Calcutta, and finally established a
palatial school in India, and a heavenly home in
America, with thousands of followers.

I share these things, not to indulge in self-praise, but in order to demonstrate that the above suggestions came from the heart of my own successful experience, and not from theories about success. I hope that if a weak and humble person like myself can accomplish something with which to serve his brethren, you, who are perhaps stronger than I was in the beginning, can surely do something for your success that will also include the success of others.

Wisdom Gem

MOST PEOPLE LIVE almost mechanically, uncon-
scious of any ideal or plan of life, and without any
apparent knowledge of spiritual truth. You must
never forget that an important part of your equip-
ment is your purpose in life. The whole world
stands aside for the person who knows where he
is going and is determined to get there. When you
have resolved definitely upon a purpose in life,
you must make everything serve that purpose.

Renunciation

One time in America, Paramhansa Yogananda met a man who was unkempt, filthy, and seemingly indifferent to what anyone thought of him (though quite possibly this was a pose intended to shock others, which of course would have shown definite interest in their opinions!). Yogananda asked him, "Why do you appear like that?"

"I'm a renunciate!" announced the other, proudly.

"But you've become attached in a new way," the Master replied, "—to disorder!"

Wisdom Gem

CLEANLINESS IS AN outward reflection of an ordered mind. When someone keeps his person clean—either his body or his clothes—it is an indication of self-respect as well as of regard for the feelings of others.

Shortbread From the
Divine Mother

ho, really, can fathom God? He is impersonal—yes, clearly so. Yet He dwells in every one of
us, and He *does* care for each of us very personal-
ly, if we give to Him our hearts. His impersonality
consists in wanting nothing from us, except, indeed
—since in each of us, through our human feelings,
He is also very personal—He longs for our love!

Sweet, foolish sentiments don't win Him.
Earnest, complete self-offering does. True miracles are a constant feature of the spiritual life. By
appealing to the Mother of the Universe, people
do receive Her loving response. The condition for
forming this relationship with Her is utter, childlike trust, and a total absence of selfish desire.

Let me finish this discussion with a very little, but true, story from the life of Paramhansa
Yogananda.

Living as he did in California, he often traveled back and forth between his headquarters
on Mount Washington, in Los Angeles, and his
oceanside hermitage a hundred miles to the south,

in Encinitas. In Laguna Beach, a little town on the way, he found a shop that made delicious Scotch shortbread. A true master like him is not attached to pleasures, and isn't driven by any slightest desire for them. Nonetheless, he can *enjoy* things. When he is strong in his non-attachment, he has no need to remain forever grimly aloof from everything.

With that preamble, I may relate that he sometimes broke his journey between Los Angeles and Encinitas by stopping at that little shop. In the car, afterward, he would share with his companions the pleasure of eating this shortbread. It was something that he enjoyed sharing especially with the Divine Mother.

One day they stopped at this shop, and a disciple went in to buy a little supply of the shortbread. She came out to report, regretfully, that all the shortbread had been sold. The Master, as he told us later, was not disappointed: he was only surprised. He never did anything without first consulting the Divine Mother. Had She, this one time, misled him?

"Divine Mother," he prayed for an instant, "what happened?"

Just then he beheld a shaft of light descend onto the roof of that shop. A moment later the proprietor ran out, bearing in her hand a little package. "Wait!" she cried. "Don't go away! This package is for you. I was saving it for another customer who had ordered it, but I can make him another batch."

Wisdom Gem

STRANGE TO SAY then, in this vast, impersonal universe where God seems remote, untouched, immutable, and apparently unconcerned, the old truths are being reinforced as it were with a vengeance! Young people, nowadays especially, want a religion that will satisfy the demands of common sense. When all the reasoning has been done, however, and the final tally is in, we find that in spite of everything the universe is more loving, more caring, more interested in us than even our forefathers believed!

Standing Up!

Years later, during the Depression years, he gave a lecture in New York. Certain rich people were taking advantage of poor ones who lacked the means even to protect themselves. In his lecture, Yogananda spoke out very strongly on the subject. He actually named a few names, accusing those he named of causing great suffering to others.

After the lecture, several people warned him, "Don't go back to the station alone. Let a few of us, at least, accompany you."

"I'm not afraid," he said. "God is with me."

He was in a dark alley, approaching Grand Central Station, when he felt a gun in his back. A menacing voice said, "Why did you say such things against those people?"

Yogananda turned around and confronted his assailant face to face. "God," he said, "is as much in His poor children as in His rich ones. And He is not pleased when the rich ones take advantage of the poor." Imagine speaking like that to someone who is pointing a gun at you!

Yogananda then gazed at the man with the spiritual power of Bliss. Suddenly, the other began to tremble violently. His pistol fell to the ground.

"What are you doing to me?" he cried. "I was sent to shoot you!"

"You can never win," Yogananda told him. "Pick up your gun."

"I can't go back to my old ways!" cried the other. Then, terrified of what had happened, he ran away into the night.

Wisdom Gem

WHEN FEAR COMES, tense and relax, and exhale several times. Switch on the electricity of calmness and nonchalance. Let your whole mental machinery wake up and actively hum with the vibration of will. Then, harness the power of will to the cogwheels of fearless caution and good judgement. Continuously revolve these to produce practical ideas for escaping your specific, impending calamity.

The Boy Who Became a Saint

In my school in India, there was a boy who was brought in by his parents. We used to take only children under twelve years of age, but he was much older. I told him he could stay on one condition—that he was willing to be good.

I had a heart-to-heart talk with him and said: "You have made up your mind to smoke, but your parents do not want you to smoke. You have succeeded in defeating your parents, but you have not succeeded in defeating your own misery. You are hurting yourself."

My arrow had struck home, and he began to weep. He said, "They are always beating me."

I said, "Think of what you are doing to yourself. Come on, I will take you, on one condition —that I will not be a detective, but your friend. As long as you are willing to correct your mistakes, I will be your helper, but if you tell lies, I will do nothing for you. Lying destroys friendship. Do not lie to me."

I accepted him and said, "Anytime you want to smoke, I will get you cigarettes."

One day, he came to me and said, "I feel a terrible desire to smoke." I offered him money, and he could scarcely believe his eyes. He said, "Take back the money." He did not want it. I was pushing him to go and buy the cigarettes, but he would not go. At last, after this tug-of-war, he said, "You will not believe me, but I no longer want to smoke."

The result of all the teaching and discipline was that he finally became a saint. I roused his spiritual consciousness. The greatest of all spiritual consciousness lies in the inner effort to go upstream toward lasting happiness. Very few people are making the effort. However, you can make a constant effort to become good, even if your sins are as deep as the Atlantic Ocean.

Wisdom Gem

THROUGH A FEW incarnations you have been a human being, but through eternity you have been a child of God.

The Man with the Nervous Heart

ome time ago a man suffering from a chronic nervous heart came to me for healing. He said, "I have tried many things, but I am unable to get rid of my heart trouble."

After calm, intuitive reflection, I told him to bring me a pair of scissors. Alarmed and suspicious, he stared at me, and remonstrated, "Sir, are you going to perform an incision on my heart?!" I laughed and replied, "I am not a doctor, and you have never heard of anyone using scissors for operating upon the heart."

When he reluctantly brought the scissors, I cut off one of his vest buttons and told him not to replace the button and not to touch the place where the missing button belonged. I asked him to come back after fifteen days, and told him I expected him to be healed by that time.

The man laughingly exclaimed, "I will do what you say, since I believe in you, but of all the crazy cures, I think this is the craziest."

After fifteen days he came to me, shouting with joy, and said, "The specialists say I am healed of my nervous heart. Sir, what did you do? Did you dispossess the button of a ghost?"

With a smile I said, "Yes, I did! Your hand was constantly fiddling with the vest button near your heart. This button was the "ghost" nagging your heart into a nervous fit. Your heart, freed from the disturbing vest button has ceased to trouble you."

Wisdom Gem

IF ONE IS nervous and keeps his body in constant motion, his Life Force is restless, his mind is restless, his vitality is restless, and his breath is restless. But if one controls the Life Force by spiritual exercises and the practice of calmness through meditation, then his mind and vital power are within his control.

The Power of Prayer

O n 14th January, 1936, Guruji went on a pilgrimage to the holy Ganga Sagar festival. Hundreds of pilgrims from all over India attend once a year just at this time. Ganga Sagar is situated 80 miles south of Calcutta, where the river Ganges meets the sea, the Bay of Bengal.

I was very fortunate to accompany Guruji to that pilgrimage. My parents opposed my going to Ganga Sagar, as the place is too cold at that time of the year, but as Guruji loved me so much, he said to my parents, "Hare Krishna must come with me." In that group my cousin sister, Amiya, her mother Subarnalata, my aunt Ashalata, Guruji's friend Tulsi Bose and his wife, (lovingly called "Martan Ma" by those who knew her), and a few other distant relatives also accompanied Guruji.

Early in the morning we boarded a big steamship, along with hundreds of pilgrims from all over India. After sailing forty miles by the river Ganges where the river was very wide and the two sides of the shore could be seen faintly, suddenly we found the ship was going down, down, down little by little into the waters, and the waters were coming up on the decks of the ship. At this all the pilgrims were frightened and running all over the decks out of fear. Even the captain of the ship was afraid. Many pilgrims seeing our Guruji clad in a saffron-colored robe, came running to him and requested him to save their lives. Guruji said, "Be calm, don't worry, and don't run out of fear. Everything will be alright. Sit down where you are and pray to God for your lives."

So the pilgrims became calm and began to pray to God. After some five or ten minutes we found the waters of the river went down from the decks and the ship came out of the water to its normal level. Then again the pilgrims came to Guruji and said, "Guruji, you have saved our lives!" But Guruji said, "No, I have not saved your lives. You prayed to God and so God has saved all our lives."

This was again a miracle for me. Everyone was relieved of the tension of being drowned. After this incident we safely arrived at Ganga Sagar. Then the captain also came to Guruji and said, "Guruji, my voice is choked since a long time. I consulted many doctors but no one could cure me. I cannot shout and command my sailors." Saying this he was trying to come near and touch Guruji's feet for his blessings. But Guruji said, "You need not come near me. I bless you. You will be cured." The next day, when we were returning back home by the same boat, we found the captain shouting at the top of his voice, commanding his sailors. With a smile Guruji said to me, "Hare Krishna, see the captain's voice is all right now."

Wisdom Gem

PRAY WITH UTTER confidence that He is listening. For indeed, so He will, if you pray to Him with love. Pray from your heart, with deep intensity.

Demand of Him lovingly; never beg. By demand I don't mean you should try to force your will on Him, as though anticipating His reluctance to accede to your wishes. I mean, pray with the firm conviction that He wants to give you everything you need, and that He will give it.

Utter faith, and love: these are the most important elements of prayer.

This Place Feels Like Home

⟨ornamental flourish⟩

During his transcontinental tour in 1924, many would have been thrilled for Swami Yogananda to make his home in their cities. But to every such invitation he replied, "My soul calls me to Los Angeles." Years later, a guest at Mt. Washington asked him, "Which do you consider the most spiritual place in America?" "I have always considered Los Angeles the Benares of America," the Master replied.

To Los Angeles he came. People flocked to his lectures in unprecedented numbers even for that city, noted as it is for its fascination with matters spiritual. Weeks passed in unceasing public service. And then he informed his delighted students that he planned to establish his headquarters there.

Numerous properties were shown to him. None, however, corresponded to the visions he had received in India. He continued his search.

In January 1925 he was out driving one day with two or three students, including Arthur Cometer, a young man who, with Ralph, another student, had chauffeured the Master across America. They drove up winding Mt. Washington Drive. As they passed Mt. Washington Estates the Master cried out, "Stop the car!"

"You can't go in there," his companions protested. "That's private property!"

But Yogananda wasn't to be dissuaded. He entered the spacious grounds, and strolled about them in silence. At last, holding onto the railing above the tennis courts, he exclaimed quietly, "This place feels like home!"

As it turned out, the property had recently been put up for sale; there were others already who wanted to buy it. But Yogananda knew it was destined to be his. So certain was he, in fact, that he invited all his students in southern California to a dedication ceremony on the still-unpurchased land. During a speech that day he informed them, "This place is yours."

The price of the property was $65,000. The Master was on the very point of signing the purchase agreement when his hand froze into immobility. "God held my hand from signing," he told me years later, "because He wanted me to have the property for less money." A few days afterwards another real estate agent was found who agreed to negotiate terms. The seller consented to come down to $45,000, provided that the sum be paid in full at the time of purchase, and that that date be set no later than three months from the day Yogananda signed the agreement. The price, though excellent, represented a lot of money, particularly in those days, when the dollar had a much higher value than it does today. When Yogananda's students learned that he had been given only three months to raise the entire sum, their interest waned noticeably. One lady exclaimed in dismay, "Why, it would take you twenty years to raise that much money!"

"Twenty years," replied the Master, "for those who *think* twenty years. Twenty months for those who think twenty months. And *three* months for those who think three months!"

He acquired the money in three months. The story of how he did so illustrates wonderfully the power of faith.

There was a student of the Swami's, a Mrs. Ross Clark, whose husband some months previously had contracted double pneumonia. The man's doctors had said he couldn't live. "Oh yes he will live," declared the Master when Mrs. Clark turned to him for help. Going to her husband's bedside, he had sat there and prayed deeply. The man was cured. Thus it was that when Mrs. Clark learned of the Master's dilemma, she told him, "You saved my husband's life. I want to help you. Would you accept a loan of $25,000 without interest for three years?" *Would* he!

"Other money," he told me, "began pouring in from our centers around the country. Soon we had another $15,000, making $40,000 in all. But the final purchase date was approaching, and we still lacked $5,000 of the total price. I wrote Mrs. Clark again to see if she could help us with this amount. Regretfully she answered, 'I've done all I can.' I thanked her once more for the enormous help she had already given. But where was that help going to come from?

"At last just one day remained! The situation was desperate. If we didn't get those five thousand dollars by noon the next day, we would forfeit our option."

Master chuckled, "I think Divine Mother likes to keep my life interesting!

"I happened to be staying in the home of someone who was rich, but insincere. He could easily have helped us had he been so inclined, but he made no move to do so. I was battling with God, 'How do You plan to give me that money before noon tomorrow?'

"'Everything will be all right,' said my host soothingly.

"'Why do you say that?' I demanded. I knew the money would come, but God needs human instruments, and this man had shown no intention of serving in that capacity. He left the room.

"Just then a gust of wind turned my face toward the telephone. There I saw the face of Miss Trask, a lady who had come to me twice for interviews. A voice said, 'Call her.' I did so at once, and explained my predicament to her.

"After a pause she said, 'Somebody just the other day returned a loan I made him years ago. I never expected to get it back. It was for $5,000! Yes, you may have it.'

"Silently I offered a prayer of thanks. 'Please,' I urged her, 'be at Mt. Washington Estates tomorrow before noon.'

"She promised to come. But by noon the next day she hadn't yet arrived! Several prospective buyers were waiting like wolves. One was telling everyone he planned to turn the place into a movie school. But the seller announced, 'We will wait the rest of the day.'

"Minutes later Miss Trask arrived. The drama was over. We paid the full purchase price, and Mt. Washington was ours!"

Thus was founded the international headquarters of Self-Realization Fellowship, the institution through which Paramhansa Yogananda disseminated his yoga teachings throughout the world.

Wisdom Gem

MAN MUST DO his best, of course. His best, however, will be crowned with success to the extent
that he realizes that it isn't he, as a human being,
who is acting, but God who is acting through him,
inspiring and guiding him.

The power that is in you is your own, but God-
given. Use it: God won't use it for you. The more
you attune your will, during activity, to His infinite will, the more you will find His power and
blessing strengthening and guiding you in everything you do.

Universal Language

(J)ne early morning, in the month of
September, Sri Yukteswarji came to our house at
4 Garpar Road. At his advice we arranged for a
Nagar Sankirtan that morning. Nagar Sankirtan
means marching on different roads by many devotees singing devotional songs, with different musical instruments carried with them.

On that day, this musical procession was led
by Sri Yukteswarji and Guruji. Many devotees, including myself, my uncle, and my father and other
relatives, were following them singing devotional
songs. We made many rounds of different streets,
and after some time we came to a certain locality
which was inhabited by people of another religion.
As we were passing through that area, we found a
furious man brandishing a stick over his head and
shouting, "Stop the music! Stop the songs!" We
stopped in fear and stopped singing. Still the man
was very furious.

At this point Sri Yukteswarji told Guruji,
"Yogananda, you go to that man and see what

is wrong with him." We were more afraid and thought, "What will happen to our Guruji if he goes to that angry man?" But without any hesitation Guruji stepped forward and stood before that man and said, "What is the matter with you? Why are you so angry? We believe in all religions and are not disturbing anyone; we are only singing our devotional songs." As soon as Guruji uttered these words, we found that angry man totally changed then and there. That man apologized to Guruji and said, "I am sorry. You may proceed and carry on with your devotional songs." We started our songs and marched past him.

Wisdom Gem

IF YOU TREAT others unkindly, you will receive
unkindness in return, both from others and from
life. Your own heart, moreover, will grow shriv-
eled and dry. Thus does Nature warn people that
by unkindness they do injury to their inner Self.

When we know what the law is and conduct
ourselves accordingly, we live in lasting happiness,
good health, and perfect harmony with ourselves
and with all life.

Untouched

The Master's spiritual power was something many could feel, emanating from him. It was something that few ever really understood.

In Philadelphia once, he was standing on a street corner when three men came before him brandishing pistols.

"Give us all your money!" they growled.

Yogananda reached into his pocket and pulled out a wad of dollar bills. "I'm happy to give you this," he said to them. "But I have another treasure inside me that you'll never be able to take from me."

The men glanced at one another sideways. "What's the matter with this guy? Is he crazy?"

"You'll never be able to rob me of my inner peace." He then looked at them penetratingly. Suddenly they began to tremble.

"Hey, listen! We don't want your money. We don't want nothing!" With those words they handed his money back to him and ran off as if for their very lives.

Wisdom Gem

As LONG AS you enjoy living and acting in this dream of delusion, so long will you go on, for incarnation after incarnation, experiencing the pains and pleasures of this world and this body. The Bhagavad Gita describes it as a great wheel, endlessly turning. If, however, you desire strongly to get out you must be released. Remember, freedom is your eternal destiny."

Visions and Phenomena

People have a very distorted notion of what the spiritual path is all about," Yogananda said. "Visions and phenomena aren't important. What matters is complete self-offering to God. One must be absorbed in His love.

"I remember a man who came forward after a lecture in New York and claimed that he could enter cosmic consciousness at will. Actually, what he meant was that he could travel astrally, but I saw right away that his experiences were imaginary. Still, I couldn't simply tell him so; he wouldn't have believed me. So I invited him up to my room. There I asked him to favor me by going into cosmic consciousness.

"Well, he sat there fidgeting, eyelids flickering, breath heaving—signs, all, of body-consciousness, not of cosmic consciousness! At last he could contain himself no longer.

"'Why don't you ask me where I am?'

"'Well,' I said, to humor him, 'where are you?'

"In rounded tones, as if hallooing from a

Stories from the Life of Yogananda

distance, he replied: 'On top of the dome of the Taj Mahal!'

"'There must be something the matter with your own dome!' I remarked. 'I see you sitting fully here, right in front of me.' He was utterly taken aback.

"I then made a suggestion. 'If you think you can travel all the way to the Taj Mahal in India, why not see if you can go somewhere nearby, to test the validity of your experience?' I suggested that he project himself to the hotel dining room downstairs, and describe what he saw there. He agreed to the test. Going into 'cosmic consciousness' again, he described the dining room as he saw it. He actually believed in his visions, you see. What I wanted to do was demonstrate to him that they were the products of a vivid power of visualization. He described a number of things in the restaurant, including a group of people seated in a corner farther from the door.

"I then described the scene as I saw it. 'In the right-hand corner,' I said, 'there are two women seated at a table by the door.' I described a few more things as they were at the moment. We went downstairs at once, and found the room as I had described it, not as he had. At last he was convinced."

Wisdom Gem

EVERY PATH TO God has its own pitfalls. The special pitfall on the path of *raja yoga* is the temptation to spiritual pride as a result of one's meditative insights or new-found miraculous powers. The most important thing to bear in mind is that what truly matters is not what God is giving you, in terms of visions and consolations, but rather what you are willing of yourself to give Him. Don't seek experiences for their own sake nor be attached to them. As Yogananda said, "The path to God is not a circus!"

We Are All a Little Bit Crazy and Don't Know It

T he iron horse "Chief" was racing over the tracks with its noisy hoofs carrying us off fast in its gorgeous Pullman cars. I was seated in my assigned section, peering through the window, watching the mountains, trees, and landscapes flit by. Opposite me sat an Ego-inflated movie actor, wearing a face painted with sarcasm and pity. He seemed to be "condescending" to sit opposite me, a Hindu with long flowing hair and an orange robe. He gave me an indirect look or two of mystic disgust, almost openly signifying that I had no business confronting him in such a strange attire. Due to my clean-shaven face and long flowing hair, he was comparing me to some strange woman imported from the Orient. Anyway, his face writhed more and more into a look of agonized disgust when he saw that I was looking at him with an unperturbed gaze.

Suddenly, I hurled a few words at him. With soft audacity I demanded: "Mister, will you please tell me why you have assumed such a harried expression?"

"None of your business", he angrily replied. He was about to leave when, like the firm hand of a mother's love curbing a wayward child, I caught hold of his hand and commanded him to sit down, saying that I wanted to talk to him, please.

He automatically and helplessly sat down, re-marking: "You are the most audacious person I have ever met during my travels." I paid no atten-tion to his remarks, but he sulkily repeated: "And it's none of your business what kind of an expres-sion I have."

"Of course it is my business, sir, to tell you about your self-distorted face, as I have to look at it steadily for many hours. Won't you please paint a rosy smile over your dark, gloomy face?"

At this remark, he smiled from ear to ear, his well-formed, well-polished teeth partially show-ing. My movie friend, by his smile signified: "Hostilities have ceased, now state your intention quickly and in as few words as possible."

Finding him in a receptive mood, I started: "Well, my friend, it was an accident that you were born an American and I was born a Hindu, but I know that you and I are both God's children, now and always. Before we leave this earth, we shall have to drop our mortal titles and know ourselves only as God's children."

"Yes, I know all that," was the bland, dry reply.

I, with unabated warm enthusiasm, in spite of the cold blanket of indifference which he cast over me, continued: "Brother, do you know that in this world we are all a little bit crazy and don't know it?"

"Why, what do you mean?" countered my new acquaintance. He apparently did not care to agree that he was crazy too.

Paying no attention to his question, I went on: "Do you know why people can't find out their own craziness?"

"Why don't they?" was the childlike inquiry.

By this time I could see that he was becoming more receptive to my words. Then I went on: "Well, you know people don't detect their own craziness because crazy people of the same feather flock together.

"It is true that material business men, professors, lawyers, spiritual monks, and so on, like their own kind. If I were a movie actor, then we would have at least tolerated each other; and if I had met another Hindu with my tastes instead of meeting you, then we would perhaps have had a jolly good time. But as it is, I have the advantage because I know about your craziness as a movie actor, and you don't know anything about my craziness. Well, I promise you, it is a very interesting occasion because you have the chance of a lifetime to prove the truth that: When people differently crazy come together, then they find out about their own craziness."

My movie actor friend was jolted from his pedestal of sarcasm, lost control of his guarded manner, and burst into a long, loud laugh adding: "That is well said!"

But I wasn't through with him yet. I made him promise to listen carefully to me. "I know about your craziness for movies, but you don't know about my craziness," I went on. "Here is one chance in eternity to learn the details concerning my form of craziness and then find out whether mine will afford more real happiness than yours, or vice versa."

Before our long discussion started, I warned him against stubborn wandering arguments by enjoining: "Remember, fools argue, while wise men discuss." I made him feel that he and I were too wise to make such a mistake. So he raised no protest when I asserted: "Mr. Movie Actor, if I can convince you by logic that my God-craziness is better than your movie craziness, then you must follow me; but if you can talk me into believing that yours is better than mine, then I will be a movie actor."

Well, I am not a movie actor yet, for my friend lost out and followed me instead.

The fact is, we must not dislike people because they are different from us, or because their opinions differ from ours. We are almost crazily determined to believe in our own pet self-formulated convictions. Since we of the East and the West don't know about each other's particular craziness, it is best that we come together and point out to each other our specific beliefs.

When the East remarks on the West's craziness for material possessions, and when the West, in a friendly way, points out the spiritual one-sidedness of the East, then each will remove its one-sidedness, and both will constructively exchange experiences for a balanced civilization after the pattern of God's Cosmic Plan.

Wisdom Gem

EVERY DAY TRY to help uplift physically, mentally, or spiritually suffering people, as you would help yourself or your family. If, instead of living in the misery-making selfish way, you live according to the laws of God, then, no matter what small part you may be playing on the stage of life, you will know that you have been playing your part correctly, as directed by the Stage Manager of all our destinies. Your part, however small, is just as important as the biggest parts in contributing to the success of the Drama of Souls on the Stage of Life. Make a little money and be satisfied with it by living a simple life and expressing your ideals, rather than make lots of money and have worries without end.

Index:
Stories Listed by Their
Spiritual Qualities

Index:
Spiritual Qualities Listed by Their Stories

Bibliography

Ghosh, Hare Krishna. 2022. "The Power of Prayer." *Thank You, Master: Direct Disciples Remember Paramhansa Yogananda*, 22–23. Nevada City: Crystal Clarity Publishers.

Ghosh, Hare Krishna. 2022. "Universal Language." *Thank You, Master: Direct Disciples Remember Paramhansa Yogananda*, 23–24. Nevada City: Crystal Clarity Publishers.

Kriyananda, Swami. 2011. "A Changed Life." *Paramhansa Yogananda: A Biography*, 79. Nevada City: Crystal Clarity Publishers.

Kriyananda, Swami. 2011. "Called to America." *Paramhansa Yogananda: A Biography*, 60. Nevada City: Crystal Clarity Publishers.

Kriyananda, Swami. 2011. "Fads, Diets, Science, and Common Sense." *Paramhansa Yogananda: A Biography*, 88. Nevada City: Crystal Clarity Publishers.

Kriyananda, Swami. 1990. "Faith vs Carelessness / Grace vs Self-Effort." *The Essence of Self-Realization: The Wisdom of Paramhansa Yogananda*, 105. Nevada City: Crystal Clarity Publishers.

Kriyananda, Swami. 1990. "Money Won't Give You Happiness / The Folly of Materialism." *The Essence of Self-Realization: The Wisdom of Paramhansa Yogananda*, 2. Nevada City: Crystal Clarity Publishers.

Kriyananda, Swami. 2011. "My Experience with an Orthodox Believer in Hell-Fire." *Paramhansa Yogananda: A Biography*, 83. Nevada City: Crystal Clarity Publishers.

Kriyananda, Swami. 2011. "Never Call Yourself a Sinner." *Paramhansa Yogananda: A Biography*, 82. Nevada City: Crystal Clarity Publishers.

Kriyananda, Swami. 2004. "Overcoming Anger." *Conversations with Yogananda*, 176–179. Nevada City: Crystal Clarity Publishers.

Kriyananda, Swami. 2006. "Renunciation." *The Essence of the Bhagavad Gita: Explained by Paramhansa Yogananda*, 490. Nevada City: Crystal Clarity Publishers.

Kriyananda, Swami. 2006. "Shortbread From the Divine Mother." *The Essence of the Bhagavad Gita: Explained by Paramhansa Yogananda*, 440. Nevada City: Crystal Clarity Publishers.

Kriyananda, Swami. 2011. "Standing Up!" *Paramhansa Yogananda: A Biography*, 90. Nevada City: Crystal Clarity Publishers.

Kriyananda, Swami. 2002. *The Art and Science of Raja Yoga*. Nevada City: Crystal Clarity Publishers.

Kriyananda, Swami. 2010. "I Am God." *The Bhagavad Gita Talk*, Episode 45.

Kriyananda, Swami, ed. 1990. *The Essence of Self-Realization: The Wisdom of Paramhansa Yogananda*. Nevada City: Crystal Clarity Publishers.

Kriyananda, Swami. 1999. *The Light of Superconsciousness: How to Benefit from Emerging Spiritual Trends*. Nevada City: Crystal Clarity Publishers.

Kriyananda, Swami. 1977. "This Place Feels Like Home." *The Path*, 186-190. Nevada City: Crystal Clarity Publishers.

Kriyananda, Swami. 2011. "Untouched." *Paramhansa Yogananda: A Biography*, 80. Nevada City: Crystal Clarity Publishers.

Yogananda, Paramhansa. 1938. "A Bunch of Grapes." *Praecepta Lessons*, Vol 4, #91.

Yogananda, Paramhansa. 2015. "A Great Failure Who Became a Great Success." *How to Awaken Your True Potential*, 71–75. Nevada City: Crystal Clarity Publishers.

Yogananda, Paramhansa. 1938. "Death and the Dream." *Praecepta Lessons*, Vol 3, #76-77.

Yogananda, Paramhansa. 1938. "Ever-New Joy." *Praecepta Lessons*, Vol 4, #92.

Yogananda, Paramhansa. 2011. *How to Achieve Glowing Health and Vitality.* Nevada City: Crystal Clarity Publishers.

Yogananda, Paramhansa. 2008. *How to Be a Success.* Nevada City: Crystal Clarity Publishers.

Yogananda, Paramhansa. 2006. *How to Be Happy All the Time.* Nevada City: Crystal Clarity Publishers.

Yogananda, Paramhansa. 2010. *How to Have Courage, Calmness, and Confidence.* Nevada City: Crystal Clarity Publishers.

Yogananda, Paramhansa. 1938. "Mistaken Identity." *Praecepta Lessons*, Vol 4, #89.

Yogananda, Paramhansa. 1938. "My Pet Deer." *Praecepta Lessons*, Vol 4, #97.

Yogananda, Paramhansa. 1938. "Open Your Bank Book with God." *Praecepta Lessons*, Vol 5, #129.

Yogananda, Paramhansa. 2008. "Path of Success: A Personal Account." *How to Be a Success*, 99-100. Nevada City: Crystal Clarity Publishers.

Yogananda, Paramhansa. 2015. "The Boy Who Became a Saint." *How to Awaken Your True Potential*, 37–38. Nevada City: Crystal Clarity Publishers.

Yogananda, Paramhansa. 1934. "We Are All a Little Bit Crazy and Don't Know It." *Praecepta Lessons*, Vol 1, #17.

Yogananda, Paramhansa, and Swami Kriyananda. 2017. "The Man with the Nervous Heart." *The Man Who Refused Heaven: The Humor of Paramhansa Yogananda*, 52–53. Nevada City: Crystal Clarity Publishers.

Yogananda, Paramhansa, and Swami Kriyananda. 2017. "Visions and Phenomena." *The Man Who Refused Heaven: The Humor of Paramhansa Yogananda*, 31–32. Nevada City: Crystal Clarity Publishers.

About the Storyteller — Author Paramhansa Yogananda

"As a bright light shining in the midst of darkness, so was Yogananda's presence in this world. Such a great soul comes on earth only rarely, when there is a real need among men."

—HIS HOLINESS THE SHANKARACHARYA
OF KANCHIPURAM

Born in 1893, Yogananda was the first yoga master of India to take up permanent residence in the West.

Yogananda arrived in America in 1920 and traveled throughout the country on what he called his "spiritual campaigns." Hundreds of thousands filled the largest halls in major cities to see the yoga master from India. Yogananda continued to lecture and write up to his passing in 1952.

Yogananda's initial impact on Western culture was truly impressive. But his lasting spiritual legacy has been even greater. His *Autobiography of a Yogi*, first published in 1946, helped launch a spiritual revolution in the West. Translated into more than a dozen languages, it remains a best-selling spiritual classic to this day.

Before embarking on his mission, Yogananda received this admonition from his teacher, Swami Sri Yukteswar: "The West is high in material attainments but lacking in spiritual understanding. It is God's will that you play a role in teaching mankind the value of balancing the material with an inner, spiritual life."

In addition to the *Autobiography of a Yogi*, his spiritual legacy includes music, poetry, and extensive commentaries on the Bhagavad Gita, the Rubaiyat of Omar Khayyam, and the Christian Bible, showing the principles of Self-realization as the unifying truth underlying all true religions.

Widely considered one of the 20th century's most influential spiritual teachers, his life and work helped launch and inspire a spiritual revolution. By the turn of the century, thousands of seekers around the world considered themselves his disciples.

Further Explorations

Crystal Clarity Publishers

If you enjoyed this title, Crystal Clarity Publishers invites you to deepen your spiritual life through many additional resources based on the teachings of Paramhansa Yogananda. We offer books, e-books, and audiobooks, a wide variety of inspirational and relaxation music composed by Swami Kriyananda, and yoga and meditation videos.

See a listing of books below or visit our secure website for a complete online catalog, or to place an order for our products.

crystalclarity.com | clarity@crystalclarity.com

14618 Tyler Foote Rd. | Nevada City, CA 95959

800.424.1055

Ananda Worldwide

Crystal Clarity Publishers is the publishing house of Ananda, a worldwide spiritual movement founded by Swami Kriyananda, a direct disciple of Paramhansa Yogananda. Ananda offers resources and support for your spiritual journey through meditation instruction, webinars, online virtual community, email, and chat.

Ananda has more than 150 centers and meditation groups in over forty-five countries, offering group-guided meditations, classes and teacher training in meditation and yoga, and many other resources.

In addition, Ananda has developed eight residential communities in the US, Europe, and India. Spiritual communities are places where people live together in a spirit of cooperation and friendship, dedicated to a common goal. Spirituality is practiced in all areas of daily life: at school, at work, or in the home. Many Ananda communities offer internships where one can stay and experience spiritual community firsthand.

For more information about Ananda communities or meditation groups near you, please visit ananda.org or call 530.478.7560

The Expanding Light Retreat

The Expanding Light is the largest retreat center in the world to share exclusively the teachings of Paramhansa Yogananda. Situated in the Ananda Village community near Nevada City, California, it offers the opportunity to experience spiritual life in a contemporary ashram setting. The varied, year-round schedule of classes and programs on yoga, meditation, and spiritual practice includes Karma Yoga, personal retreat, spiritual travel, and online learning. Large groups are welcome.

The Ananda School of Yoga & Meditation offers certified yoga, yoga therapist, spiritual counselor, and meditation teacher trainings.

The teaching staff has years of experience practicing Kriya Yoga meditation and all aspects of Paramhansa Yogananda's teachings. You may come for a relaxed personal renewal, participating in ongoing activities as much or as little as you wish. The serene mountain setting, supportive staff, and delicious vegetarian meals provide an ideal environment for a truly meaningful stay, be it a brief respite or an extended spiritual vacation.

For more information, please visit expandinglight.org or call 800.346.5350

Ananda Meditation Retreat

Set amidst seventy-two acres of beautiful meditation gardens and wild forest in Northern California's Sierra foothills, the Ananda Meditation Retreat is an ideal setting for a rejuvenating, inner experience.

The Meditation Retreat has been a place of deep meditation and sincere devotion for over fifty years. Long before that, the Native American Maidu tribe held this to be sacred land. The beauty and presence of the Divine are tangibly felt by all who come here.

Studies show that being in nature and using techniques such as forest bathing can significantly reduce stress and blood pressure while strengthening your immune system, concentration, and level of happiness. The Meditation Retreat is the perfect place for quiet immersion in nature.

Plan a personal retreat, enjoy one of the guided retreats, or choose from a variety of programs led by the caring and joyful staff.

For more information or to place your reservation, please visit meditationretreat.org, call 530.478.7557, or email meditationretreat@ananda.org

The Original Writings of Paramhansa Yogananda

1946 Unedited Edition of a Spiritual Masterpiece

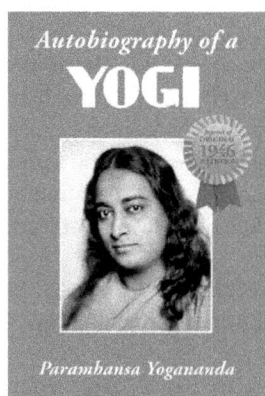

AUTOBIOGRAPHY OF A YOGI
Paramhansa Yogananda

Autobiography of a Yogi is one of the world's most acclaimed spiritual classics, with millions of copies sold. Named one of the Best 100 Spiritual Books of the twentieth century, this book helped launch and continues to inspire a spiritual awakening throughout the Western world.

Yogananda was the first yoga master of India whose mission brought him to live and teach in the West. His firsthand account of his life experiences in India includes childhood revelations, stories of his visits to saints and masters, and long-secret teachings of yoga and self-realization that he first made available to the Western reader.

This reprint of the original 1946 edition is free from textual changes made after Yogananda's passing in 1952. This updated edition includes bonus materials: the last chapter that Yogananda wrote in 1951, also without posthumous changes, the eulogy Yogananda wrote for Gandhi, and a new foreword and afterword by Swami Kriyananda, one of Yogananda's close, direct disciples.

Also available in Spanish and Hindi from Crystal Clarity Publishers

SCIENTIFIC HEALING AFFIRMATIONS

Paramhansa Yogananda

Yogananda's 1924 classic, reprinted here, is a pioneering work in the field of self-healing and self-transformation. He explains that words are crystallized thoughts and have life-changing power when spoken with conviction, concentration, willpower, and feeling. Yogananda offers far more than mere suggestions for achieving positive attitudes. He shows how to impregnate words with spiritual force to shift habitual thought patterns of the mind and create a new personal reality.

Added to this text are over fifty of Yogananda's well-loved "Short Affirmations," taken from issues of *East-West* and *Inner Culture* magazines from 1932 to 1942. This little book will be a treasured companion on the road to realizing your highest, divine potential.

METAPHYSICAL MEDITATIONS

Paramhansa Yogananda

Metaphysical Meditations is a classic collection of meditation techniques, visualizations, affirmations, and prayers from the great yoga master, Paramhansa Yogananda. The meditations given are of three types: those spoken to the individual consciousness, prayers or demands addressed to God, and affirmations that bring us closer to the Divine.

Select a passage that meets your specific need and speak each word slowly and purposefully until you become absorbed in its inner meaning. At the bedside, by the meditation seat, or while traveling — one can choose no better companion than *Metaphysical Meditations*.

~ WISDOM STORIES series ~

Yogananda knew that stories have a way of opening our hearts and minds, making connections the intellect alone may miss. He told these tales to illustrate the spiritual and practical truths he was teaching. Not only to be inspired but also able to apply those teachings to our daily lives. Each individual story in this series, is followed by a "Wisdom Gem," illuminating spiritually vital qualities such as Right Action, Courage, Unconditional Love, Faith, and Wisdom, in an enjoyable way to explore and reflect on these universal principles.

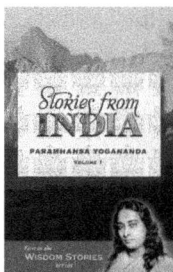

STORIES FROM INDIA, VOLUME ONE
Paramhansa Yogananda

Paramhansa Yogananda's treasury of Indian tales will delight both the casual reader and students of Eastern thought. Featuring a gamut of characters-from saints to thieves, God-realized masters co lions and frogs-these stories were all told by the Master himself in his lectures, informal talks, and writings.

Whether you are a teacher, parent, student, or devotee, these stories are an excellent resource to turn to again and again for inspiration, sharing, and personal study.

STORIES FROM INDIA, VOLUME 2
Second in the Wisdom Stories series
Paramhansa Yogananda

As a universal medium, stories reach into the hearts of all God's children — young and old — delivering timeless truths in ways easy to digest and assimilate. Perhaps, more than anything, this is why Paramhansa Yogananda wove stories into all of his teachings through his lectures and books and why his close disciple, Swami Kriyananda, did the same.

This second volume in the Wisdom Stories series picks up where volume one left off with stories shared by the great yoga master, Paramhansa Yogananda (author of the spiritual classic and best-selling title *Autobiography of a Yogi*) and his close direct disciple, Swami Kriyananda. These stories have been recounted for generations and imparting universal values of compassion and understanding, virtue, *dharma* (right action), and the ability to relate to another's reality.

Selected Offerings

THANK YOU, MASTER
Hare Krishna Ghosh, Meera Ghosh, and Peggy Deitz

Anyone who has read and loved *Autobiography of a Yogi* will be delighted to find this treasure of personal experiences and heartfelt remembrances of Paramhansa Yogananda by three of his direct disciples.

Stories from Yogananda's family members, Hare Krishna Ghosh and Meera Ghosh, who became disciples as teenagers, take the reader on pilgrimage to India to the sacred places and miraculous moments shared with this great yogi. The stories of Peggy Deitz transport one to Yogananda's ashram in California and his time living with devotees in America.

Whether humorous or miraculous, casual or divine, these accounts bring to life the experience of being in Yogananda's presence. They give insight into the profound love with which he guided each individual.

Firsthand experiences from close disciples are a true gift that can help us tune into his vast nature. At the same time, these delightful stories will touch your heart and uplift your spirit.

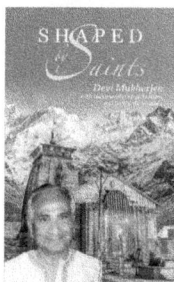

SHAPED BY SAINTS
Devi Mukherjee

While a young man, Devi Mukherjee worked with Mahatma Gandhi in the Indian resistance movement and was imprisoned for five months. After his release, Devi began a spiritual quest throughout India, traveling some forty-five years at various times.

From 1955–66, he was part of the Yogoda Satsanga Society, Yogananda's organization in India. There, he and Swami Kriyananda were brother monks. He later married the daughter of Yogananda's childhood friend Tulsi Bose. The Mukherjee family lived in Tulsi's former house in Calcutta, where he and Yogananda dreamed and meditated as boys.

Devi takes the reader on a profoundly inspiring pilgrimage to meet saints and realized masters of modern India in forest ashrams, mountain caves, holy places, and shrines. He shares many insights and lessons from the great ones and tells many previously unpublished stories of Yogananda's early life and return visit to India in 1935–36.

PARAMHANSA YOGANANDA
A Biography with Personal Reflections and Reminiscences
Swami Kriyananda

Paramhansa Yogananda's life was filled with astonishing accomplishments. And yet in his classic autobiography, he wrote more about the saints he'd met than about his own spiritual attainments. Yogananda's direct disciple, Swami Kriyananda, relates the untold story of this great master and world teacher: his teenage miracles, his challenges in coming to America, his national lecture campaigns, his struggles to fulfill his world-changing mission amid incomprehension and painful betrayals, and his ultimate triumphant achievement. Kriyananda's subtle grasp of his guru's inner nature reveals Yogananda's many-sided greatness. Includes many never-before-published anecdotes and an insider's view of the Master's last years.

THE ESSENCE OF SELF-REALIZATION
The Wisdom of Paramhansa Yogananda
Recorded, compiled, and edited by his disciple, Swami Kriyananda

Filled with lessons, stories, and jewels of wisdom that Paramhansa Yogananda shared only with his closest disciples, this volume is an invaluable guide to the spiritual life carefully organized into twenty main topics.

Great teachers work through their students, and Yogananda was no exception. Swami Kriyananda comments, "After I'd been with him a year and a half, he began urging me to write down the things he was saying during informal conversations." Many of the three hundred sayings presented here are available nowhere else. For anyone wishing to know more about Yogananda's teachings and absorb his wisdom, this book and *Conversations with Yogananda* are must-reads.

Be assured that at each sitting, whether for one page or one chapter, you will have gleaned some refreshment for a tired heart or a thirsty soul. . . . *Essence* is easy to read, besides being quite a bit of fun. —*Spirit of Change Magazine*

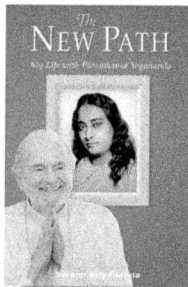

THE NEW PATH
My Life with Paramhansa Yogananda
Swami Kriyananda

The New Path is a moving revelation of one man's search for lasting happiness. After discarding the false promises offered by modern society, J. Donald Walters found himself (much to his surprise) at the feet of Paramhansa Yogananda, asking to become his disciple. How he got there, trained with the Master, and became Swami Kriyananda make fascinating reading.

The rest of the book is the only complete account of what it was like to live at the feet of that great man of God—one who was destined to bring major changes to the world.

Anyone hungering to learn more about Yogananda will delight in the hundreds of stories of life with a great avatar and the profound lessons they offer. This book is an ideal complement to *Autobiography of a Yogi*.

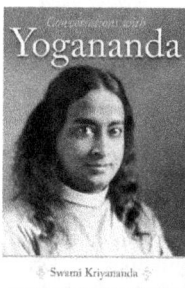

CONVERSATIONS WITH YOGANANDA
Recorded, with reflections, by his disciple,
Swami Kriyananda

For those who enjoyed Paramhansa Yogananda's autobiography and hunger for more, this collection of conversations offers rare intimate glimpses of life with the Master as never before shared.

This is an unparalleled account of Yogananda and his teachings written by one of his closest disciples. Swami Kriyananda was often present when Yogananda spoke privately with other close disciples, received visitors and answered their questions, and dictated and discussed his writings. He recorded the Master's words, preserving a treasure trove of wisdom that would otherwise have been lost.

These conversations include not only Yogananda's words as he spoke them but the added insight of a disciple who has spent over fifty years attuning his consciousness to that of his guru.

The collection features nearly five hundred stories, sayings, and insights from the twentieth century's most famous master of yoga, as well as twenty-five photos—almost all previously unreleased.

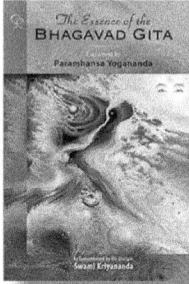

THE ESSENCE OF THE BHAGAVAD GITA

Explained by Paramhansa Yogananda

As remembered by his disciple, Swami Kriyananda

Rarely in a lifetime does a new spiritual classic appear that has the power to change people's lives and transform future generations. This is such a book. This revelation of India's best-loved scripture approaches it from a fresh perspective, showing its deep allegorical meaning and down-to-earth practicality. The themes presented are universal: how to achieve victory in life in union with the Divine; how to prepare for life's "final exam," death, and what happens afterward; and how to triumph over all pain and suffering.

The book itself is a triumph. Swami Kriyananda worked with Paramhansa Yogananda in 1950 while the Master completed his commentary. At that time, Yogananda commissioned him to disseminate his teachings worldwide.

"Millions will find God through this book!" Yogananda declared upon completion of the manuscript. *"Not just thousands — millions. I have seen it. I know."*

GOD AS DIVINE MOTHER

Wisdom and Inspiration for Love and Acceptance

Paramhansa Yogananda and Swami Kriyananda

We long for a God who loves us exactly as we are, who doesn't judge us but rather helps and encourages us in achieving our highest potential. In this book, discover the teachings and inspirations on Divine Mother from Paramhansa Yogananda. These teachings are universal: No matter your religious background, or lack thereof, you will find these messages of love and acceptance resonating on a soul level.

"The role of the Divine Mother is to draw all Her children, all self-aware beings everywhere, back to oneness with God."

In this book, you will discover: Who is Divine Mother?; How to develop the heart's natural love; What attitudes draw Her grace; How to tune in to Divine Mother. Included also are over thirty poems and prayers dedicated to God in the form of Divine Mother, as well as original chants and songs by the authors.

WHISPERS FROM ETERNITY
A Book of Answered Prayers
Paramhansa Yogananda
Edited by his disciple, Swami Kriyananda

Many poetic works can inspire, but few have the power to change lives. These poems and prayers carry extraordinary power, having been "spiritualized" by Paramhansa Yogananda: Each has drawn a response from the Divine. Yogananda was not only a master poet whose imagery here is still as vivid and alive as when first published in 1949: He was a spiritual master, an avatar.

He encouraged his disciples to read from *Whispers from Eternity* every day, explaining that through these verses he could guide them after his passing. But this book is not for his disciples alone. It is for spiritual aspirants of any tradition who wish to drink from this bountiful fountain of pure inspiration and wisdom.

SONGS OF THE SOUL
Paramhansa Yogananda

Yogananda preferred to express his wisdom not in dry intellectual terms but as pure, expansive feeling. To drink his poetry is to be drawn into the web of his boundless, childlike love. In one moment his *Songs of the Soul* invite us to join him as he plays among the stars with his Cosmic Beloved. Then they call us to discover that portion of our own hearts that is eternally one with the Nearest and Dearest. This volume is a bubbling, singing wellspring of spiritual healing that we can bring with us everywhere.

~ THE WISDOM OF YOGANANDA series ~

In this series, Yogananda offers timeless wisdom in an approachable, easy-to-read format. The writings of the Master are presented with minimal editing, to capture his expansive and compassionate wisdom, his sense of fun, and his practical spiritual guidance.

HOW TO BE HAPPY ALL THE TIME, VOLUME 1

Yogananda explains everything needed to lead a happier, more fulfilling life: looking for happiness in the right places; choosing to be happy; tools, techniques, and methods for achieving happiness; sharing happiness with others; and balancing success with happiness.

KARMA AND REINCARNATION, VOLUME 2

Yogananda reveals the reality of karma, death, reincarnation, and the afterlife. With clarity and simplicity, he makes the mysterious understandable: why we see a world of suffering and inequality; what happens at death and after death; the purpose of reincarnation; and how to handle the challenges we face in our lives.

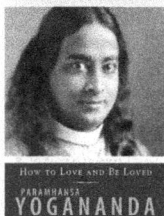

HOW TO LOVE AND BE LOVED, VOLUME 3

Practical guidance and fresh insight on relationships of all types are shared by Yogananda: how to cure friendship-ending habits; how to choose the right partner; the role of sex in marriage; how to conceive a spiritually oriented child; the solutions to problems that arise in marriage; and the Universal Love at the heart of all relationships.

HOW TO BE A SUCCESS, VOLUME 4

The Attributes of Success, Yogananda's original booklet on reaching one's goals, is compiled with other writings on success: how to develop habits of success and eradicate habits of failure; thriving in the right job; how to build will power and magnetism; and finding the true purpose of one's life.

HOW TO HAVE COURAGE, CALMNESS, AND CONFIDENCE, VOLUME 5

A master at helping people change and grow, Yogananda shows how to transform one's life: dislodge negative thoughts and depression; uproot fear and thoughts of failure; cure nervousness and systematically eliminate worry from life; and overcome anger, sorrow, oversensitivity, and a host of other troublesome emotions.

HOW TO ACHIEVE GLOWING HEALTH AND VITALITY, VOLUME 6

Yogananda explains principles that promote physical health and overall well-being, mental clarity, and inspiration in one's spiritual life. He offers practical, wide-ranging, and fascinating suggestions on having more energy and living a radiantly healthy life. Readers will discover the priceless Energization Exercises for rejuvenating the body and mind, the fine art of conscious relaxation, and helpful diet tips for health and beauty.

HOW TO AWAKEN YOUR TRUE POTENTIAL, VOLUME 7

With compassion, humor, and deep understanding of human psychology, Yogananda offers instruction on releasing limitations to access the power of mind and heart. Discover your hidden resources and be empowered to choose a life with greater meaning, purpose, and joy.

THE MAN WHO REFUSED HEAVEN, VOLUME 8

Why is humor so deeply appreciated? Laughter is one of the great joys of life. Joy is fundamental to who we are. The humor in this book is taken from Yogananda's writings. Also included are experiences with the Master that demonstrate his playful spirit.

HOW TO FACE LIFE'S CHANGES, VOLUME 9

Changes come not to destroy us, rather, to help us grow in understanding and to learn the lessons we must to reach our highest potential. Guided by Yogananda, tap into the changeless joy of your soul-nature, empowering you to move through life fearlessly and with an open heart. Learn to accept change as the reality of life; face change in relationships, finances, and health with gratitude; and cultivate key attitudes like fearlessness, non-attachment, and willpower.

HOW TO SPIRITUALIZE YOUR LIFE, VOLUME 10

Yogananda answers a diverse range of questions asked by truth-seekers, sharing his teachings and insights on how to be successful in the everyday world and in one's spiritual life. Addressing financial, physical, mental, emotional, and spiritual challenges, he explains how best to expand one's consciousness and live life to the fullest. Compiled from his articles, lessons, and handwritten letters, this tenth volume in the Wisdom of Yogananda series was written in a question-and-answer format, well suited to both individual and group study.

HOW TO LIVE WITHOUT FEAR, VOLUME 11

Yogananda said that one of the greatest enemies of willpower is fear. Avoid it both in thought and in action. Fear doesn't help you to get away from the object of fear, it only paralyzes your willpower. Here the great yoga master, Paramhansa Yogananda, teaches us how to: eliminate the mental bacteria of fear, rid the mind of worry poisons, overcome stage fright, use chants and affirmations to overcome fear, and much more!

HOW TO INCREASE YOUR MAGNETISM, VOLUME 12

What is the secret power that the world's winners possess? Can you get more of it for yourself? Can it help you overcome your challenges in your work, in your relationships, in your health, and on the battlefield of daily life?

Yogananda introduced an approach to personal development that rests on a foundation of timeless ancient truths adapted for our present, scientifically curious age of energy-awareness. You can use these teachings now to: Magnetize Your Body & Mind; Become Magnetic with Radiant Joy; Overcome the Obstacles to Magnetism; Increase Your Abundance & Success Magnetism; Use Faith, Hope, & Love to Make You More Magnetic; Magnetize Your Soul.